SOUTHERN INTERIORS

THE GREEN DRAWING ROOM—THE NATHANIEL RUSSELL HOUSE

The Drawing Room—The Colonel John Stuart House

SOUTHERN
Interiors

of *Charleston*
SOUTH CAROLINA

The Colonel William Rhett House

BY

Samuel Chamberlain
and
Narcissa Chamberlain

EDITED BY NARCISSE CHAMBERLAIN

HASTINGS HOUSE, *Publishers*   NEW YORK

MANTEL DETAIL

The Gaillard-Bennett House

LIBRARY OF CONGRESS CATALOG CARD NUMBER :   56-12014

Historic Charleston is a city of multiple charms, any one of which might be the theme of a book. Its half-hidden gardens, for example, provide a subject full of surprises and beauty . . .

The tradition of fine decorative ironwork is firmly established in Charleston. Architects and draftsmen have long since joined forces to publish illustrated volumes about it . . .

Visitors who stroll down these venerable streets are captivated by old buildings, so remarkably reminiscent of Europe. A photographic essay on Charleston's smiling exteriors would be picturesque...

And finally, Charleston is a city of enchanting vistas to tempt the discriminating camera. Ignoring such blandishments with difficulty, the lens behind this book is focused on another, and more intimate subject, the interiors beyond Charleston's hospitable thresholds . . .

4

A TABLE OF CONTENTS

FOREWORD

The city of Charleston, South Carolina—to paraphrase a familiar epigram about Boston —is less a place than a way of life. To an extraordinary degree the grace of Southern living has persisted in this peninsula city; the warm climate, the relaxed pace and the tradition of "three o'clock dinner" combine to preserve the charm of the past on this historic strip of land embraced by the Cooper and the Ashley Rivers. The city is something of a phenomenon. In spite of war, bombardment, flood, hurricane, pestilence and earthquake, it has probably retained more of its beauty than any Colonial city on the continent. Because the earliest houses have been destroyed by a variety of disasters—and because of the sad economic plight of the South after the War between the States, when building activity practically ceased—most of the old residences which remain fall into the Georgian and Federal periods, the latter defined locally as "Adam." This poverty, which prevailed throughout much of the late 19th century, brought with it a certain blessing, for it kept out the scourge of Victorian architecture and furniture which afflicted more prosperous communities.

The grandeur of early 19th-century living may have disappeared, but Charleston still clings to a reasonable facsimile, still retains its own individuality and aroma. High-ceilinged drawing rooms with crystal chandeliers and damask hangings, mahogany sideboards glistening with family silver, formal gardens and broad verandas—these are still the hallmark of Charleston, despite the noisy intrusion of this mechanistic century.

Today the graceful Charleston way of life excites a great deal of admiration among travelers who come to the peninsula city in ever-increasing numbers, particularly in the early spring. The chill, uncompromising month of March, unwelcome in most parts of these United States, is kind to Charleston. Eager Northerners and sun-tanned sybarites from Florida join in a mass invasion at this enchanted moment when the sun is bright, the air is cool, and the flowers are at their peak of beauty. It is then that Charleston's three famous gardens, Magnolia, Cypress and Middleton, aflame with azaleas and camellias, are besieged by visitors. A generous surge of hospitality makes itself felt in the time-honored city. It extends beyond gardens, churches, museums and shops, too, right across the thresholds of Charleston's exquisite old houses. For a period of several weeks, guided tours through these stately homes of Charleston become one of the city's most gratifying attractions. Church and garden clubs arrange many of these tours, but the most active organization in this field has been the admirable Historic Charleston Foundation. Through its efforts, the beauty of Charleston's interiors is revealed to thousands of genuinely interested people each year.

The fortunate visitor who is guided through a good cross-section of Charleston houses comes away enchanted, his mind crowded with cherished impressions. The composite picture of so much ancestral furniture, sensitive architecture, subtle color and skillful wood-carving is memorable. But, due to the frailties of the human mind, it is also forgettable. A book illustrating these and many other old Charleston interiors should provide a welcome reminder for this faintly befuddled visitor, and should prove to be a precious document to less fortunate beings who must visit the city through the printed page, not to mention architects, decorators and antiquarians. This was our thought after taking the tour and finding one small guidebook to be the best and only souvenir available.

The bibliography of Charleston, however, is awe-inspiring, even alarming, in its completeness and especially so to new writers venturing on the scene. Could there possibly be justification for another book on this much-treated area? Certainly it would be presumptuous to write of Charleston's history, or its personalities, even its architecture and gardens. All of them have had gifted, well-documented interpreters. But on one theme, strangely enough, there seemed to be room for embellishment. A careful search of available books convinced us that an illustrated volume depicting Southern interiors as they exist in old Charleston and in the surrounding Low Country would be very much in order.

The result is primarily a book of pictures. This does not aspire to be a history, even though a good deal of the city's rich past creeps into the captions. The story is told with carefully composed photographs, taken indoors and out and pointed up with a tailored text. However, there are gaps in a narrative form of this kind, and it is the object of this Fore-

word to fill some of them and to sketch at least the basic background of Charleston's historic architecture.

Charleston was founded on its present site shortly after 1669, under a grant from King Charles II. The Carolinas, a tract then stretching presumably to the Pacific Ocean, were given to a group of the King's favorites, known as the Lords Proprietors, to colonize and exploit as they wished. Planters came here from the Barbados; French Huguenots arrived seeking religious freedom; and in time groups of other nationalities landed, among them English Puritans, Germans, Dutch, Scotch-Irish and Swiss.

The colonists were soon protesting the rule of the overbearing Lords Proprietors who turned deaf ears to their complaints and ignored their protests against injustices. In 1719 the revolt was complete and the colony became a province of the Crown. A class of prosperous planters grew up in this romantic Low Country, so well suited to the cultivation of rice and, in some parts, of indigo and cotton. These wealthy families maintained close relations with the mother country and usually sent their sons to be educated in English schools and universities. They became a power within the colony, contributing many statesmen, soldiers, ambassadors and governors to its history. A group of planters, interrelated by marriage, built some of the stateliest mansions in the whole country on their plantations along the Ashley River, and here they developed show-gardens which became famous the world over. Some of these properties are still in the possession of their descendants and the gardens built by past Draytons and Middletons at Magnolia and Middleton Place are visited by thousands of tourists each year.

Most of the wealthy planters built imposing town houses in Charleston as well, thus escaping the hot, malarial plantation lands in summer. Here they could enjoy the comparatively cool breezes from the sea and the gay social life of the city, where living developed on a scale probably more elegant than in any other community on the eastern seaboard.

The outward aspect of Charleston, so intensely individual, is something of a national curiosity. The southern European air of the city is due largely to its climate, semi-tropical vegetation, high brick walls and the use of colorful stucco surfaces. Its closed and hidden gardens, tall wrought iron gates, its steep tile roofs and delicately designed balconies all bring to mind the ancient cities of the Mediterranean. Its trees hung with Spanish moss, the negro flower sellers and the tall spires of its famous churches, St. Philip's and St. Michael's, are familiar to countless people who have never even visited the city.

From the time of its founding, the architectural styles of Charleston have been predominantly English, although considerable French influence came in with the Huguenots. Many carpenters, joiners, and masons came here from England and placed their advertisements in the 18th-century issues of the *South Carolina Gazette*. Unfortunately, architects and builders rarely signed their names to the early buildings, so little is known of the actual designers of most of Charleston's famous houses. But they were men of consummate good taste. There are superb examples of Georgian architecture in Charleston to prove the fact. They built mostly in brick, for stone was a rarity. As time went on, styles changed, of course, passing through a rococo period which reflected Chippendale design and culminating in what most authorities classify as the Federal style.

As the name implies, this period in American architecture fell at a time when we were no longer a group of English colonies, but an independent country of federated states. The influence of the brothers Adam was strong in the Federal period, and particularly so in Charleston. This was due largely to the enthusiasm of Gabriel Manigault, Charleston's most celebrated amateur architect. The Manigaults were a French Huguenot family from La Rochelle who prospered and became prominent in the city. Gabriel traveled and studied in Europe and brought back a number of books on architecture with him. His ardor for the Adam style was intense, and his houses were among the few which incorporated the curving rooms and large bays so dear to the brothers Adam. But it was the delicate Adam detail which made the greatest conquest. In fact, it became such a rage that Charleston was in danger of being completely swamped in nymphs, cupids and floral swags. Stucco-mold details became so popular that old Georgian mantels were supplanted by Adamesque versions at an alarming rate. Most 18th-century mansions in the city now reveal the change at a glance. A stuccoworker named William Purvis is responsible for much of the best decoration at this time. The Adam period lasted through the first two decades of the 19th century, when the Greek revival gradually took over as the dominant influence.

Most Charleston houses are classified as "single" or "double." The majority are single houses, presenting a narrow front to the street and extending deeply into shady gardens at the back, where often a detached kitchen, old slave quarters and carriage houses still stand. Along the side wall, usually facing south, runs a two-story "piazza" or gallery, perhaps a questionable architectural embellishment, but most agreeable and functional in this hot, sunny climate. The famous piazzas may have been introduced as early as 1700, coming from the West Indies. At first they had but one story, appended to higher brick buildings, but they developed further, as shady traps for the sea breezes, and a commodious two- or three-story gallery is now a standard Charleston institution.

The entrance to the single house is midway along the piazza and leads to a central hall. Living and dining rooms are at each side. Upstairs, there is usually a formal drawing room on the street front. Because of the low level of this peninsula, "where the Cooper and the Ashley Rivers meet to form the Atlantic Ocean," Charleston's basements are built above ground. The street ends of these ground floors were often used as offices or shops. The important rooms were on the second floor to receive the blessing of the breeze.

These tall, slender houses, often three stories high and capped by a dormered roof, seem ungainly at first to the untutored eye. Their form was imposed on the builders by the long, narrow lots originally laid out in the "Grand Modell" under the Lords Proprietors, and by the fact that many of the lots were split into even smaller frontages as building increased on the narrow peninsula. When the eye becomes more accustomed to the single house and one perceives that house, garden, piazza and outbuildings are all happily integrated for indoor and outdoor living, the plan becomes logical and attractive.

The "double" house usually has the same central-hall plan, but its wide façade faces the street instead of being placed at right angles to it. Its central doorway is often approached by a double flight of steps, and the house is usually two rooms deep instead of one. Both types of Charleston house are repeatedly illustrated in the pages which follow.

Charleston's wealth in architecture and in noble interiors is truly fabulous. We would not intimate for a moment that *all* the fine houses of Charleston are included in the fifty-one houses illustrated in this volume. They certainly are not, but on the other hand, *most* of them are. Practically all of those which are open to the public in springtime are included, and there are many others which are never revealed to any but family and friends.

The orderly arrangement of such a wealth of photographic material presented something of a problem. Should the houses appear chronologically, or in order of elegance, or by locality? The problem was finally solved by dividing the heart of the book into seven chapters, each concerned with a different segment of Charleston's architectural inheritance. Four of these chapters take the reader on a conducted stroll along four of Charleston's most gracious streets—Meeting, Church, Legare and Tradd, with occasional side excursions. A fifth chapter leads from South Battery along the Bay Shore to the colorful Rainbow Row. The scattered houses north of Broad Street fail to fall into an itinerary, but they make a sixth chapter full of interest. Finally, a few of the neighboring plantations, without which a treatise on Charleston would be quite incomplete, are grouped together to bring the book to a close.

This volume should serve as a tribute to another phase of Charleston life—the kindness and generosity of its citizens. To obtain these protographs it was necessary to make a mass assault on the good nature and privacy of Charlestonians which has had few parallels in recent years. They could not have been more cooperative, or more hospitable. If we had been named the Samuel Rutledge Ravenels, our welcome could not have been more sincere, and our first word of thanks goes to the dozens of patient people who allowed us to invade their homes armed with cameras, tripods, floodlights and notebooks.

Of the more than 1400 photographs which we took, only 314 are reproduced in the book. The stern demands of limited space have caused some agonizing omissions, including six houses which we photographed only to find that there was no room left for them in the final layout. To those owners who received us so well, and whose houses are *not* reproduced, we tender particular thanks.

Any number of warm-hearted individuals helped us in this agreeable task. Our gratitude goes out especially to a soft-spoken young dynamo whose name is Frances Smythe Edmunds, and whose first concern, after her thriving family, is the Historic Charleston Foundation. It was Mrs. Edmunds who served as our sponsor and fairy godmother in Charleston. Then there is a triumvirate of generous and erudite Charlestonians who are invariably sought out by fact-hungry visitors and who are more than generous with their time, talent, and wisdom. To E. Milby Burton, Director of the Charleston Museum, Albert Simons, F.A.I.A., and Samuel Gaillard Stoney, outgiving experts on Charleston furniture, architecture, and history respectively, we express our warm appreciation. Finally, to our daughter Narcisse, whose editorial gifts have been of incalculable help, go our beaming thanks.

SAMUEL AND NARCISSA CHAMBERLAIN

LIST OF HOUSES ILLUSTRATED

MEETING STREET

The Branford-Horry House

This pilgrimage to the old houses of Charleston begins on a sunny morning on Meeting Street with one of the finest double houses in the city, built in about 1751 by William Branford. In the Charleston idiom, this imposing residence is called "double" because it has two rooms, rather than one, as well as its entrance door, all facing the street. The portico, extending boldly over the public way, was built in the 1830's by Elias Horry, great-grandson of the original builder. Beyond are the twin towers of the First (Scotch) Presbyterian Church.

(Opposite) Architects will be delighted by the wealth of Georgian woodwork throughout this house. In the downstairs drawing room is an impeccable mantel whose egg-and-dart, bolection and fine dentil moldings were certainly assembled by an exceptional craftsman. The figurines are, from left to right, 18th-century Meisson, Chelsea (*c.* 1770), and French. The covered jar is one of a Chelsea Derby pair.

The four walls of the downstairs drawing room are finished in deeply beveled paneling. The portrait is of the owner's great-grandfather, Chief Justice Benjamin Faneuil Dunkin. The fireplace grate and the two rows of Sadler tiles came from an English house of the same period at Bath.

The library is completely paneled in South Carolina cypress from which all the paint has been stripped. Wine-red velvet hangings at the windows complement the warm tan of the rubbed wood. The chimney pieces throughout the house are imaginatively varied and this one is of an exceptional key-stone design. Audubon's son painted the landscape over the mantel in the province of Matanzas, in Cuba. He gave it to Justice Dunkin, who had helped him finance his Cuban trip.

The stately hall doors were probably widened by Elias Horry in the 1820's. They open here into the downstairs drawing room whose tremendous Chinese rug is over a century old. The set of Hepplewhite chairs and settee is a fine copy of considerable age. The chandelier and the painted chairs in the hall came from Justice Dunkin's Waccamaw River Plantation.

In the downstairs drawing room, porcelains and miniature silver from the owner's large collection are arranged on a Chippendale table at the left. Spode and Worcester decorate the Queen Anne table (*c.* 1740) in the corner.

This graceful Empire table with carved dolphin supports still shows traces of its original gold decorations. Charmingly grouped with it are porcelains, an American banjo clock (*c.*1810), and tiny miniatures and medals.

The Branford-Horry House

The Sheraton dining room table, seen from the hall, was made at the plantation of the owner's great-great-grandfather. On the Empire sideboard are a George III silver tea set and a replica (*c.*1830) of a cruet stand made by Paul Revere for Peter Faneuil of Boston.

An arched door leads from the second-floor hallway into the upstairs drawing room. A single glance at the paneled fireplace wall of this room is enough to explain why it has been called one of the most distinguished 18th-century rooms in America. The experts still disagree about whether woodwork of this time was always painted, or whether it was sometimes left bare to show its natural beauty, but it is impossible not to be charmed by the warmth and magnificence of this native cypress woodwork from which every sign of paint has been painstakingly removed. The soft tone of the cypress is accented, perhaps intentionally, with a design of darker pieces of mahogany and tulipwood in the carved pilasters, fretwork and decorated moldings. It is possible, however, that these other woods were used simply because their texture is especially suitable for carving. The whole of this wall is original and unspoiled. The arched, paneled door is flanked by fluted Corinthian pilasters, an idea which was used very soon again in other Charleston houses, as was the formal arrangement of short pilasters on each side of the overmantel.

The brown and apple-green upholstery of the contemporary sofa and armchair, and the faded salmon-pink satin curtains (*above,* seen through the arched doorway) are an inspired combination of texture and color against the natural wood of this remarkable room.

The Branford-Horry House

18

The Branford-Horry House   The carving of the architrave and bolection molding, and the workmanship of the classic details above them indicate that a master hand took part in the construction of this house. The mantel ornaments consist of a girandole candelabrum and Staffordshire and Rockingham figurines.

The Timothy Ford House

This house is one of several built in Charleston by Northerners. Timothy Ford, of New Jersey, prospered here when he came to practice law after his graduation from Princeton. He indulged in the luxury of two successive Charleston wives and built this house, in about 1800, for the second one. Much entertaining took place within it hospitable walls. Timothy Ford was host here to Lafayette on the General's memorable return visit to this country in 1824. This is a characteristic "single" house, one room deep on the street side, with the entrance door leading from the street into a piazza on the garden side. Wisteria masks the shady porches and smothers the fence with a natural screen to protect the privacy of the garden.

(Opposite) This arrangement on a table in the downstairs drawing room is a delectable exercise in wit and color. The remarkably detailed Dresden group in the center represents a well-bred little 18th-century *bacchanale*. The silk under it is embroidered in tones of deep apricot, green and gold. On either side are a pair of silver candlesticks, delicate silver salts on tripod bases, and small silver trays. The English print above is gravely entitled "Love's Pleading."

The ivory walls of the dining room are symmetrically designed with arched wall cupboards, recessed windows and a simple mantelpiece. Some of the owner's fine china collection is seen here: blue Canton in the cupboards and Chinese export plates and vases on the mantel.

LOVE'S PLEADING.

This house shows the Adam influence which became so popular in Charleston toward the end of the 18th century. Typical of the best of this style are the pilasters and the floral and swag decorations on the downstairs drawing room mantel, and the carved cornice molding.

The Timothy Ford House

In the upstairs drawing room, the eye of an artist planned the pale gold curtains, clear turquoise walls and notes of mulberry and petunia in the carpets and porcelains. The ribband-back Chippendale chair is a particularly fine one, upholstered in *grospoint*, as is the Chippendale armchair. The cherry highboy still has intact the original step shelves with finials.

The Timothy Ford House

The finely worked mantel in this drawing room combines incised wood carving and stucco relief decorations in the Adam manner, focusing on an elaborate floral spray on the center tablet. The two sheep and the figurine group on the mantelshelf are Staffordshire.

In the upstairs drawing room *(above)*, is a particularly graceful, early 19th-century couch with the classic lines of the period.

(Right) A small bedroom boasts a notable William and Mary highboy.

With a fine sense of scale, this symmetrical arrangement against another wall of the upstairs drawing room combines crystal wall sconces, a gilt-framed portrait and prints, lyre-backed side chairs and comfortable armchairs around a small American lowboy.

The Timothy Ford House

The Timothy Ford House

This bedroom is papered in an airy, over-all, flower-garden pattern. A fine Queen Anne table stands by a wing chair of the stame style. The side chair at the right is Sheraton, as is the graceful four-post bed, covered with rose-colored Chinese silk, in the foreground. The portrait is by the French painter Carolus Durand. The figurines are Staffordshire.

In the downstairs hall, picturesque pieces from the owner's collection: a painted Louis XVI console table, silver lyre candlesticks and a French Empire chair with a lyre-and-swan back.

Even the smaller bedrooms in the house are allotted their share of antiques, in this case a fine small field bed and a tall-case clock.

The Nathaniel Russell House

Nathaniel Russell was the son of a chief justice of Rhode Island. He came to Charleston from Bristol before the Revolution and in time became one of the most successful businessmen in the city. In Charleston, he was fondly (we assume) nicknamed "the King of the Yankees," and became president of the Charleston New England Society. He and his family lived for some time on East Bay, near the harbor, the scene of his business activities, as was customary with the merchants of this era. Quite late in life he built this truly elegant house in the Adam style on Meeting Street which had become a more fashionable residential neighborhood. It is known that he was living here by 1809 and that he spared neither pains nor money to make his house a fine one. It cost, in fact, something over $80,000. His pride as owner of the most elegant house in the city must have been somewhat humbled by the whims of weather. A newspaper of September, 1811, reports that a tornado left his house entirely unroofed, the windows broken and the furniture ruined, at a loss of $20,000. However, it was promptly restored and the family lived here until the house was sold by Russell's daughter in 1857 to a governor of South Carolina, Robert F. W. Alston. Since then it has been a convent school and the home of several owners.

This detail from the grey, oval drawing room upstairs is an example of the lavish designs in classic Adam style throughout the house. Decorations from these same molds appear again and again in Charleston houses of the period. The mantel is painted marble-white against the grey wall.

In February, 1955, the house came into the hands of the Historic Charleston Foundation. This organization of public-spirited citizens has since put it into good repair, opened it to the public as a house-museum, at the moment only partially furnished, and hopes to complete its restoration as one of the finest mansions of the Federal period in America. Sensitive brickwork with white marble trim, tall windows in recessed arches, and balconies with slender iron railings distinguish the exterior. The house is surrounded by a spacious garden protected from the street by a brick wall with railings added by a recent owner. But fine as its exterior is, the house must be examined within before the amount of careful planning and fine workmanship that Nathaniel Russell lavished upon his home can be fully appreciated.

(Right) In the hall is this remarkable free-flying staircase that swings up in sweeping curves to the third floor without touching the walls. A source of wonder to visitors, there are only one or two others comparable to it in Charleston. Light pours into the hall from windows in the stair well.

The Nathaniel Russell House   The dining room was elongated in 1908 and the cornice, wainscot and other details were identically matched with the original room. Someone in the Russell family might easily have chosen the Hepplewhite table and sideboards, the set of Sheraton chairs and the matched pair of chandeliers.

On the library mantel is a relief of the god Bacchus and his chariot against a Wedgwood-blue background. The portrait by Jarvis shows the builder at eighty-one.

Facing himself across the room in another portrait, by Edward Savage, is Nathaniel Russell at fifty-one. The Chippendale chest conceals a writing shelf.

The library walls are Pompeian red with buff woodwork. The revolving drum table of Sheraton style is flanked by 18th-century chairs of indeterminate pedigree. The globe, dated 1799, is one of a celestial and terrestrial pair, each with a compass in its base.

The Nathaniel Russell House

The garden elevation of the house shows a six-sided bay which results in fine oval rooms inside: the library *(opposite)* and this grey drawing room upstairs. Nathaniel Russell evidently lived in the grand manner, for his house has a number of imposing rooms for formal entertaining. This one, decorated in two tones of warm grey, is the most sophisticated. The carved details were originally gold-leafed. The French *vernis Martin* chairs are part of Charleston history: General Charles Cotesworthy Pinckney was sent on a mission to France by President Adams, in 1796. Shortly thereafter, he ordered two large sets of *vernis Martin* furniture from Paris. The sofas and chairs from these sets are scattered today in the Charleston homes of the descendants of his family.

The Nathaniel Russell House

The oval library creates a curved wall in the hall against which the carved cornice, doorframe and wainscoting are perfectly fitted in one unbroken curve.

On the inside of a similar wall in the grey drawing room, an intricate doorway is fitted to the curved construction. The mirror panes, also slightly curved, are original.

The Nathaniel Russell House

(*Left*) Across the front of the house, on the second floor, is another distinguished drawing room, painted two subtly different shades of green. Tall windows stretching to the floor light it from three sides and lead to balconies above the garden. The crystal teardrop chandeliers, the carving and stuccowork of the door and window frames and of the ceiling cornice, constitute one of the best Adam-inspired interiors in Charleston. The mantelpiece (see *Frontispiece*) is painted white, in imitation of marble against the darker wall. The inner facing is actually of white marble. Over the mantel hangs a painting by Angelica Kauffmann, who also did painted decoration for original Adam furniture in England.

(*Opposite*) This doorway in the green drawing room echoes precisely the formal design of the windows. Its slender recessed columns with fanciful capitals, the charming row of iris and honeysuckle in relief across the architrave, and the moldings and fretwork were designed by an imaginative architect who remains, alas, unknown.

The Daniel Huger House

The Huger House, built in about 1760, was owned for some time by Mrs. Elizabeth Blake, who may have been the original builder. Her sister was Mrs. Miles Brewton, whose distinguished house still stands nearby on King Street. Her cousin was the wife of Lord William Campbell, Royal Governor of the Province. In 1775 the Revolutionary politics of the day forced the Governor to flee. He made his precipitous exit from Mrs. Blake's house, some say via the large Palladian window in the stairway, to the end of the garden where Vander Horst's Creek then flowed. A boat took him to the harbor and the safety of the man-of-war H.M.S. Tamar. In 1795, the house was sold to Colonel William Morris of New York, whose niece and her husband, Daniel Elliott Huger, later obtained possession. Their descendants have occupied it ever since. The Huger House has the well-proportioned façade of a classic town house. Its fine interior suffered during the War between the States; traces of shell damage can still be seen in the paneling of the hall. When the city fell in 1865, the house was sacked and the great mirrors that once filled the panels of the drawing room were lost.

The big drawing room is noteworthy for its handsome cornice, the ornamental plasterwork on the ceiling, and an early overmantel with short pilasters and a broken pediment above. The mantelpiece itself is of a later period, added when Adam decoration became a fashionable habit in Charleston. Handsome today, this room must have been extraordinary with its mirrored panels.

The Daniel Huger House

The drawing room extends into a smaller room which, fortunately, was not considered important enough for drastic redecoration. Therefore, the fine Georgian mantel has never been replaced. Bronze ornaments are sharply silhouetted against the white woodwork.

The original fireplace has a curious but graceful marble insert that appears to be of French origin. Above it hangs a very fine 18th-century Italian water color.

In a bedroom, the early cornice, paneling and mantel remain as they always have been. The bedpost in the foreground is carved with a traditional rice motif.

On a small English sideboard in the dining room stand two covered Sheffield dishes, parts of a set of family plate that was safely buried during the War between the States. The English Regency chair is one of a superb set of twelve. The 18th-century portrait is of Ralph Izard, a controversial Charlestonian who conspired against Benjamin Franklin's negotiations in France.

The Daniel Huger House

The William Mason Smith House

William Mason Smith was a planter and the son of Robert Smith, the first Church of England bishop of South Carolina. He built this house in about 1820, when the fine proportion and delicacy of the Federal period were fading, but before the heaviness of the Victorian had taken over. French Empire and English Regency were the predominant influences in this country at the time. The house has high ceilings and arched windows and doors. The sweeping curve of its lovely staircase, which originally had a domed roof, was first built into a projection of the outside wall. The stair well is now covered over and made one with the rest of the house.

In the drawing room are two sofas, dating from soon after 1800, in the style of Sheraton's "Grecian couch." Made of golden curly maple, they are a part of a set of seventeen pieces, all in the house, which belonged to Thomas Bennett, Governor of South Carolina from 1820 to 1822.

The full sweep of the staircase is seen from the other end of the hall. The tall-case clock was made by the Charleston clockmaker, John Monroe. Another typical South Carolina piece is the Queen Anne table (*c.* 1740) on the right, with straight legs and club feet.

The William Mason Smith House

The John Edwards House

One of the finest houses on Meeting Street, from an architectural point of view, is this one built for John Edwards in about 1770, probably by William Miller and John Fullerton, who constructed a number of fine residences at this period. A double flight of steps with iron railings curves up from the sidewalk to a landing. The portico is supported by Ionic columns and the walls of the house are elegantly surfaced with wooden rustication. Inside and out the architectural details, predominantly Georgian, are handsomely designed. In 1793, Alexandre François Auguste, Marquis de Grasse (son of the admiral, the Comte de Grasse, who commanded the French fleet at Yorktown) arrived in Charleston with his wife and daughters, four sisters and his stepmother. They had fled from San Domingo where he was a planter, because of the native uprisings. This was the house where they found refuge, through the hospitality of John B. Holmes who then lived there. De Grasse must have had some difficulty in supporting his bevy of dependent ladies, for in the newspaper he later advertised a "school of designing," and taught architecture and landscaping, as well as the gentlemanly art of fencing.

The original dining room paneling has been rubbed down to the natural cypress, and the fireplace holds an interesting old hob grate with decorative tiles at the sides.

The moldings, fretwork, pilasters and rococo carved decoration of this chimney breast in the upstairs drawing room are all very fine. In the center panel is a recent portrait of the exterior of the house.

In the stair hall, behind the paneled front hall, is a remarkable French Empire tall-case clock with ormolu decorations. The stair itself is entirely finished in rubbed mahogany.

In the downstairs drawing room is still another good Georgian fireplace with the original paneling above it. It is flanked by two arched niches of considerably later date.

The John Edwards House

The Josiah Smith House

The historic promenade down Meeting Street ends with the Josiah Smith House. Josiah Smith is known to have reclaimed a substantial area of the swampy land that originally spread, broken with creeks and covered with moss-hung trees, south of today's Meeting Street. He probably built this post-Revolutionary house at the edge of his reclamation project in 1783. His venture sounds rather like a modern real-estate investment. At least, this lot and its house found a buyer in a certain Wilson Glover in 1800. For a number of recent years the house was the home of the Charleston Club. Today, it is in private hands again and has been handsomely refurbished. Over the years, certain changes have taken place, the woodwork in the front of the house being, for example, somewhat later than the Georgian paneling at the back.

(Right) The dining room is decorated with elegant formality. A fine old sideboard in the Hepplewhite style is placed under a regally carved and gilded Chippendale mirror.

The windows of the dining room are hung with silk damask curtains copied in detail from curtains at Thomas Jefferson's Monticello. The oval mirror on the far wall is carved in very rich Adam style. Walls, carpet and curtains are light, to contrast with dark mahogany furniture.

The stair hall, separated from the front hall by a keystone arch, is completely authentic and it is one of the finest in Charleston. The walls are covered with a beautiful contemporary Chinese paper, hand-painted in a pattern of flowering trees against a silver ground. On the floor is a succession of remarkably fine Oriental rugs.

The Josiah Smith House

CHURCH
STREET

The Thomas Legare House

Church Street is narrower and less exclusively residential than lower Meeting Street. Many of its houses are very early and they are usually not as formal as some of the great mansions of Charleston. There are shops, narrow sidewalks and flowering gardens to delight the inquiring visitor, as well as old graveyards and fine churches such as St. Philip's and the old French Huguenot Church shown on the preceding page. At the southern end of Church Street is this house built in the 1760's by Thomas Legare, member of a family of Huguenot settlers. The scale of this house is in general moderately small, and the ceilings are lower than in later houses.

(Opposite) The cypress panels in the library are rubbed down to the natural wood. The panel with "ears" over the mantel is hung with a fine girandole mirror. A brass fender and fan screen glow becomingly against the fireplace facing.

The drawing room's paneling and chimney are original. The landscape is by Joseph Aiken, brother of Governor William Aiken, an ancestor of the owner.

The woodwork of the hall and of the small, steep staircase is entirely free of paint. The paneling is cypress, the floor is pine and the handrail is mahogany.

The deep-rose damask hangings in the library are well over a century old and belonged to Joseph Aiken, as did the Simon Willard banjo clock from New England on the right. The room succeeds in looking both lived-in and decoratively in tune with its period.

The Thomas Legare House

On the simply detailed library mantel is a pair of miniatures by John Ramage of John Vander Horst, an officer in George Washington's command, and of his wife.

The front-hall girandole mirror bristles with classic ornaments: a crouching eagle, cornucopias of wheat and flowers, a lion's head, crystal-hung candle brackets.

44

The Heyward-Washington House

Charlestonians take particular pride in the Heyward-Washington House on Church Street. It is believed that an earlier house was torn down when the present one was built, in about 1770, by Daniel Heyward, a rice planter of St. Luke's Parish. The house went to his son, Thomas Heyward, who was a delegate from South Carolina to the Continental Congress and one of the signers of the Declaration of Independence. In 1791, during Thomas Heyward's ownership, the house was leased by the city and was beautifully furnished as a residence for President George Washington during his visit to Charleston. Many receptions and entertainments took place here during the week of his stay. The house is now the property of the Charleston Museum and is furnished with a wealth of fine Charleston-made furniture. It is hoped, in time, to complete the furnishings with pieces dating no later than the time of Washington's visit. The restoration plans include the service buildings in the rear — a kitchen, wash-kitchen, necessary, carriage house and tool shed, and a formal garden of the period. The house itself is a characteristic three-story, double one, practically square in plan, with a central hall and four rooms on each floor.

The panel above the Georgian mantel is trimmed with a band of mahogany fretwork. The door on the left opens into a "thoroughfare" closet and then into a room beyond. The English Georgian settee and chairs were among the original furnishings of the famous Drayton Hall Plantation.

The Heyward-Washington House

(*Above*) The upstairs drawing room is severely handsome, in the best Georgian tradition. As it is the main reception room, its decoration is the most formally elaborate in the house. The walls are completely paneled; there is a broken pediment over each door, and paneled shutters fold into the frames of the recessed windows. The cornice is coved into the ceiling above a line of fretwork on the wall. Against the north wall are a Georgian marble-topped table and chairs, again pieces from the Drayton Hall set. The clock is Charleston-made.

(*Left*) On the south wall hangs a Georgian mirror with a dramatic phoenix in the broken pediment. The glass reflects a portrait of a member of the Holmes family on the opposite wall.

(*Opposite*) The outstanding piece of furniture in the house is this monumental bookcase in the library. It belonged to John Bee Holmes, the city recorder who officially received President Washington in Charleston. Truly remarkable is the fact that it still contains its original 18th-century library, including books on politics, a series on the history of Jamaica and Dr. Samuel Johnson's two-volume *Dictionary*. The case is of mahogany elaborately inlaid with satinwood and ivory. The cypress frame and drawer linings show it to be locally made, though the cabinetmaker's name is not known.

The library has peach-colored plaster walls and paneling painted a deep green-blue. On each side of a pembroke table stand Hepplewhite chairs that were used in a New York house where Washington visited. Over the fireplace hangs a portrait of Thomas Heyward.

The Heyward-Washington House

This inlaid mahogany secretary in the library resembles the big bookcase in design, though it was probably made at a slightly later date by another craftsman.

In a bedroom is a portrait of Mrs. Daniel Heyward. The walls are buff plaster with dark, muted-green panels. The carved post of a rice bed is in the foreground.

The William Hendricks Buildings

Through an arched passage between shops on Church Street, one enters a charming paved garden that leads to this diminutive residence. The buildings on the street were tenements built as an investment by William Hendricks in 1749. This small house in the rear contained kitchens to serve them. It is a particularly appealing example of what has been done in Charleston to restore and adapt old buildings for contemporary use. The old chimney serves two huge fireplaces inside. The house contains many pieces brought back from the Orient by the owners' seafaring New England ancestors, among them Oliver Hazard Perry, hero of the battle of Lake Erie in the War of 1812, and Commodore Matthew C. Perry, who opened world trade with Japan.

In the smaller of the two living rooms hangs a portrait of Commodore Oliver Hazard Perry, painted during his lifetime. The artist's name is not known, but he was one of the masters of his time. An Imari bowl and a pair of Japanese iron candlesticks decorate the table underneath.

The big living room is a delightful mélange of East and West. The brass-bound chest is Korean, the silk temple brocade behind it is Japanese. The Hepplewhite, shield-back chair was used at the Convention that met in Philadelphia to write the Constitution.

The William Hendricks Buildings

Above the old fireplace hangs a carved ship's eagle from Nantucket. The child's chair is a very early New England piece. The polished brick floor is original.

The old kitchen beams were exposed in the living room when the low ceiling was removed. The Renaissance portrait is of the Grand Duchess of Toledo, born a Medici.

The Jacob Motte House

This tall, old double house on Church Street is impressive in scale and massive in construction, with heavy stone quoins at the corners of the walls, in the mid-18th-century Georgian manner. It was probably built shortly before 1745 by Richard Capers, member of a Huguenot family. Among it distinguished owners was Jacob Motte, Public Treasurer of the Province before the Revolution. Like so many Charleston houses, it contains any number of *bibelots* and handsome pieces of furniture that evoke the people and families of Charleston history. Mrs. William Mason Smith, whose grand-daughters live in the house today, bought it in 1869, and left in it some of its most interesting mementos: the family set of the *Encyclopedia Britannica*, published in 1806, a portrait of Bishop Robert Smith by James Earle, and the Bishop's own coconut-and-silver drinking cup. In the second-floor drawing room *(below)* is one of a pair of Mrs. Smith's very exceptional Empire card tables, made of mahogany and rosewood, with satinwood inlays. Its griffon-head harp supports are delightful curiosities of furniture-making. The painting over the mantel is of the Castle of Chillon, by Charles Fraser, great-great-uncle of the present owners.

The paneling of mote the drawing room is all original, though the cornice and mantel are later. It is still painted the color of Mrs. William Mason Smith's choice, a subtle light blue she had known in the drawing rooms of her girlhood, which she felt was "so becoming to young ladies."

The Thomas Rose House

The Thomas Rose House, built in about 1735, is usually spoken of in superlatives that it well deserves. It is an example of the earlier Georgian period at its very best. Its exterior lines are simple and solid, with quoined corners and only two floors instead of the towering three more usual in Charleston. The entrance is through the handsome portico shown here, in the end of the lower piazza that was added later. It is something of a shock for the new-comer to pass from the street through the apparently solid wall of a Charleston house, and to emerge, not in the building, but in the open air on the other side. But one soon becomes accustomed to this attractive convention and to finding the actual entrance door further on in the wall of the house. The present owners have re-stored and furnished this house with exquisite taste and care, using fine 18th-century pieces that might have been designed for it, so perfectly do they find their places there. One of their proudest, though invisible, possessions is a romantic ghost, the shade of a poetic young doctor who was killed in a duel over a young actress some two hundred years ago.

In the downstairs living room off the piazza are two Louis XV chairs covered with *grospoint*. The card tables against the far wall are American Hepplewhite, the pair of mahogany and gilt mirrors American Chippendale. A street entrance may once have been in the library beyond.

*The Thomas
Rose House*

The living room is completely paneled in its original cypress woodwork. The narrow mantelshelf holds two Delft covered jars and an elaborate French clock, a good modern copy of Louis XV style. The pole screens are made of family samplers dated 1800 and 1808. The arched wall cupboard contains part of a Crown Derby dessert set dated 1804, and Bristol-glass finger bowls.

The dining room paneling is original except for the mantelpiece and cupboard frames. The walls are light green, the cupboard linings terra cotta, echoing tones in the portrait by Benjamin West. At the left is a handsome George III silver tea urn made by Frances Crump, London, 1764.

The Thomas Rose House

This English commode, one of a pair elaborately inlaid in the Adam style, probably dates from the 1770's and is unrestored and in perfect condition.

These exquisite Royal Worcester birds are from contemporary limited editions made by the English artist Dorothy Doughty.

(Right) An arched window, masked with fitted strips of old Italian satin-stitch embroidery and fringed silk swags, lights the stairway. The small-case clock is of Irish workmanship, though the mahogany case itself is early American. The staircase is simply but meticulously finished with light panels and moldings and carved, black-walnut balusters and rail.

(Below) In a most livable and graceful fashion, the second-floor drawing room gathers together a collector's dream of original pieces. The pale cream walls, the silk damask hangings of deep peach and the lemon-gold covering of the American Chippendale sofa are all echoed in the extraordinary 16th-century Tabriz animal carpet that covers almost the entire floor. Two very fine, small Queen Anne wing chairs, upholstered in rose and white, flank the fireplace. Other chairs are a Louis XV armchair with a *grospoint* covering, American Chippendale side chairs, and in the foreground, a Hepplewhite armchair in the French manner, covered with hand-painted silk.

The Thomas Rose House

The closely-placed windows have been ingeniously curtained in an 18th-century, tapered design that avoids voluminous folds which might have overpowered the room. At the left they hang just to the level of the window seats; at the back they follow the casements to the floor.

(Above) At one end of the drawing room is a late 18th-century secretary filled with *bibelots*. Its carved cornice and the garlands and pendant husks on the glass doors suggest Adam or Hepplewhite influence.

(Left) Another view of the drawing room shows the arrangement of the fireplace wall with unsymmetrically placed arched doors. Most of the ornaments and lamps are porcelains of Chinese or English origin.

(Opposite) The English commode at the end of the room is accepted as an authentic Adam piece. The satinwood is beautifully decorated with classic painted figures, urns and garlands. The original design for this piece is found in Adam's *Works on Architecture,* inscribed "Front of a Commode in the Countess of Derby's Dressing Room." The 18th-century gilt mirror is Florentine, the decorative compotes are Directoire.

The mantel is a later replacement, but a gem of the Adam style. The carving is all wood; no stucco molds were used. The portrait is by John Berridge, 1770. The middle clock, studded with semiprecious stones, was made in 1769, in Edinborough, legend says for Marie Antoinette.

*The Thomas
Rose House*

44 Church Street

A Charlestonian with fine feeling and respect for the tradition of his city built himself this contemporary house in the style of the early residences. His gifts—and his patience—as a designer and craftsman certainly can be matched by only a small handful of today's professional cabinetmakers. With his own hand, he designed and made the carved trim of the hall (*right*), as well as much of the furniture throughout the house. In a remarkable way, the usual parallel between authenticity and sheer age does not apply to this attractive house. On its fine pieces the builder's signature and 20th-century date have a validity all their own.

The period quality of the dining room is enhanced by the original sideboard and by the table, chairs and serving table which were all made in true Hepplewhite style by the builder himself. The silver, china and prints are old, as is to be expected in this city of heirlooms.

The George Eveleigh House

At the bend where old Church Street widens into a brief tree-shaded area, stands the George Eveleigh House, older than many of its neighbors and probably built in 1738. George Eveleigh was a merchant of the early days who made much of his fortune from the deerskin trade with the Indians. The house is set well back from the street, behind a plastered brick wall with fine iron gates. The tile-paved piazza, though early, is probably not the original one, as records speak of brick pillars which were destroyed here by the hurricane of 1752. Much of the furniture in the George Eveleigh House has belonged to the same family for more generations that is usual even in Charleston. There are also numerous examples of prized Charleston-made furniture.

This Charleston-made mahogany secretary has been much admired and discussed. The brasses, handsomely shaped panels and broken pediment are particularly fine.

The four walls of the second-floor drawing room are lined with handsome, beveled cypress panels, most of them original and some of them exceptionally wide.

*The George
Eveleigh House*

Architecturally, the only late element in the drawing room is this lavish Adam mantel, replacing a marble one broken in the earthquake of 1886. It comes from the now-dismantled Nathaniel Heyward House on East Bay. The central panel, in stucco mold, shows a fox hunt.

This amusing Charleston-made gaming table has square corners for candlesticks and oval hollows for game counters. The style combines Queen Anne and Chippendale.

A detail of the mantel shows fanciful colonnettes, classic festoons, swags, and a muse with a large sea shell clinging informally to the pointed arch above her head.

19 Church Street

The owners and renovators of this pleasant retreat had a particularly happy subject with which to work. Once a carriage house and stable, it is now transformed into a residence of 18th-century style. The brick wall on the street shelters a quiet garden and a shady terrace where the carriage entrance used to be. A vine is trimmed to set off the arches of the French windows, and a wrought-iron balcony finishes the simple façade.

(*Opposite*) Old mantels such as this one in the living room are used in most of the rooms. The cornice and woodwork are meticulously finished in the same style. On the mantelshelf are Worcester Grainger potpourri jars (*c.*1845).

The gun room is built in the old horse stalls, with high stable windows still in place. The paneling and the fine Georgian-style mantel are native cypress. The Audubon print was engraved by Havell in 1834. The group of tiny birds under it were carved by Dr. George Childs.

In the dining room, brilliant 19th-century German bird prints are hung over a small English sideboard of the Sheraton style.

The living room, curtained in brown against oyster-white walls, leads to the terrace. The English armchair shows Adam influence.

The dining room is painted Williamsburg green, with windows hung in white raw silk printed in tones of green and brown. On the English mahogany table (*c.* 1780) stands one of a pair of silver tureens. On the mantel are a Crown Derby plate and a pair of miniature Worcester tureens.

The William Holmes House

This house was probably built shortly before 1809 by William Holmes, who owned the property at that time. A house that stood here earlier was destroyed by fire and only its brick service buildings remain. This view of the marble-paved piazza is unmistakably Charlestonian: the sunlit, columned piazza serves as an outdoor room, shades the interior of the house and is closed off at the far end by the street entrance. The exterior lines of the traditional Charleston piazza may not always be ideal, but it is nonetheless delightful to live with.

Large, simple panels in the drawing room set off a decorative mantelpiece in the Adam manner. The pieces of sprigged china on the mantelshelf are parts of an old French set. The semicircular side tables are a matched pair in the Hepplewhite style.

The William Holmes House

The dining room walls are very simply paneled. The chest of drawers is American Hepplewhite. The butler's tray is old and still complete with its folding stand.

In the library is another interesting old mantel with an informal design of plants and shells in the center panel. Above is an early 19th-century family portrait.

LEGARE STREET

The Simmons-Edwards House

Legare Street is one of the most tranquil of Charleston's thoroughfares, tree-shaded and relatively free of traffic. Its name, though pronounced as if "Simon" went before it, has a particular prestige among Charlestonians. Its most distinguished structure is the brick mansion built by Francis Simmons in about 1800. It was purchased, in 1816, by George Edwards, who added the brick gateposts and iron fence. The entrance, shown on the preceding page, is approached by curved, marble steps framed with iron grilles worked with Edwards' initials. The pineapple finials, symbols of hospitality, were made in Italy by workmen who seem to have been more familiar with their native artichoke than with the intended fruit. But they are handsome decoration for this dignified house of Adam design.

(Left) The furniture in the drawing room, much of it French, is arranged with an appreciative sense of color and style. In this corner, one of a pair of Louis XV console tables, possibly of Italian origin, stands under a gilt Chippendale mirror. The porcelains are a Sèvres *cachepot* and Meisson figurines.

The colors of the upholstery on these French pieces in the drawing room, the *bibelots* and silks harmonize with tones in the fine Aubusson rug. The Chippendale mirror, pair to the one above, and a French *découpage* screen with Chinese figures complete this patrician group.

The drawing room mantelpiece, with double colonnettes and classic stucco ornaments, is a notable example of the room's architectural style. The garniture is a French Empire clock and a pair of bronze and gilt candelabra. The painting is of the school of David.

The Simmons-Edwards House

The mahogany handrail of the stairway rises in an unbroken line all the way to the attic. The pattern of the French wallpaper is an authentic period design.

This skillful arrangement includes twelve French *gouaches,* depicting the months of the year, and an English Sheraton cabinet.

This view of the drawing room shows it regal proportions and its high ceilings with elaborate but delicate cornices. The bois-de-rose silk hangings echo the dominant color in the Aubusson rug. A valuable *bombé* Louis XV commode stands between two windows. Beyond is an exceptionally fine Italian marquetry desk, inlaid on all four sides.

The Simmons-Edwards House

The Simmons-Edwards House　　The stuccowork on the ceiling and on the mantelpiece in the dining room is as unerringly elegant as the detail in the rest of the house. The portrait is an early one from Dublin. The silver candlesticks of the Adam period, the English silver tankard, dated 1711, and the pair of Chinese export teapots on the mantel-shelf are all objects worthy of their handsome setting.

71

*The Simmons-
Edwards House*

(Above) On the dining room walls is a warm-grey paper printed with a French continuous design of the 1860's called *Les Quatres Ages de la Vie*. The curtains are draped in stylized folds inside the plain window frames. The generous table, the chairs and side tables are antiques of English origin.

(Left) A formal portrait and a small English Sheraton sideboard are placed in the arched and paneled niche that breaks one long wall of the room. Glittering above it and on either side are a chandelier and crystal wall sconces. The sideboard ornaments are a pair of Irish glass decanters, a pair of French Baccarat crystal candelabra, and a liqueur chest.

(Opposite) This old Dutch walnut desk in the library is a labyrinth of small drawers and pigeonholes. The center shelves display figurines of soldiers of the Napoleonic Wars, including *capo di monte* pieces bearing the Napoleonic mark. Candlesticks are placed on slides especially built for this purpose.

10 Legare Street

There are many and varied small buildings in Charleston that beg to be restored and adapted for living on a smaller scale than is possible in the big city houses. Their former purpose usually lends them the charm of the unexpected and original, as has happened in this old carriage house. It has been decorated with style, but also with a sharp eye for uncluttered practicality. In its main room, the background of low ceilings, white walls and a rugless checkerboard floor has a modern flavor against which old pieces can have their maximum effect. (*Left*) A small, early English piano by Broadwood stands at the foot of the staircase. The Currier print above shows General George Washington on a charger.

The main room is a combined living and dining room. Masking the front door is a Chinese lacquer screen, Cheng' Lung of the late 1700's, inlaid with lapis, quartz and jade. In front of it is an Italian fruitwood settee of Directoire influence with fine crossed arrows in the back.

10 Legare Street

Part of the owner's collection of prints by Currier and Currier & Ives is grouped around a canvas of Canton Harbor, painted by Sunqua in 1853. The mahogany and maple Sheraton card tables at each side of the sofa are a pair, designed with remarkably elegant and slender proportions.

A serving window opens from the living room into a thoroughly modern kitchen. The bow-front Hepplewhite chest, of mahogany and maple, is part of the owner's New England collection.

The dining table is placed by the view of the garden, seen through the arch of the old carriage door now filled in with a sheet of plate glass.

The Charles Elliott House

This spacious pre-Revolutionary house was built in about 1770 by Charles Elliott. Its original simple lines are somewhat confused by the much later piazzas, which nevertheless have a Charlestonian charm of their own. Details such as pedimented windows and strong cornices under the jutting eaves preserve much of the building's original distinction.

(Below) The dining room has simple, early paneling and abounds with old family possessions, notably a large collection of silver. The American Hepplewhite sideboard between the windows is inlaid with a pattern of grouped feathers. The fine Hepplewhite chairs, a complete set, have backs of unusual design.

The array of silver on the sideboard includes a large Georgian bowl and tea service. The two pitchers are from a monogrammed set brought to this country from Ireland by John S. Preston in the early 18th century; the massive tea urn on the table at the right is part of this set.

The Sheraton chair by this 18th-century secretary belonged to the Wade Hampton family and has a curious, urn-shaped splat.

Another fine sideboard holds a punch bowl from the Irish set and a Charleston racing trophy made for an ancestor in 1802.

One of the original pre-Revolutionary chimney breasts in an upper room was spared when later alterations were made. The wood carving in bold, high relief contains scrolls and rosettes and a curious emblem of a collared eagle's head.

Mrs. William Heyward's House

This charming double house was built in about 1789 by the widow of William Heyward, brother of Thomas Heyward who built the Heyward-Washington mansion on Church Street. Mrs. Heyward was a prosperous rice planter in her own right. It is possible that this building was originally rectangular and that the two-story, rounded bay was added soon after the house was built. Mrs. Heyward's son James, it is said, occasionally haunts this cheerful house and chooses to seat himself comfortably at the desk in the library.

The curved bay and Palladian window are outstanding features of the grey drawing room. The valences of the crimson damask curtains belonged to the owner's great-great-grandmother. The pembroke table against the window has unusual grooved legs and is probably Charleston-made. The *vernis Martin* chair in the foreground is from one of the famous Charles Cotesworthy Pinckney sets.

The library has simple paneling painted with the original graining. The portrait by Jeremiah Theus is of Colonel Daniel Horry, whose son married Lafayette's ward.

The drawing room mantelpiece is a much admired example of the late 18th-century style in Charleston, with classic stucco details and a white marble facing.

Mrs. William Heyward's House   The dining room was damaged by alterations during the 19th century, and the present attractive room is a restoration. The serving table is English Hepplewhite and the sideboard is from the family plantation. The portrait of the owner's great-great-aunt, Anna Huger, is by Flagg.

The Sword Gate House

It is not known who built the early 19th-century house behind this celebrated gateway, but many names have been associated with it. Among them is that of Madame Talvande, a refugee from San Domingo, who kept a girls' school here. A member of her family is thought to have laid out the original gardens. George A. Hopley, a British consul, bought the house in 1849, and apparently it was he who installed these handsome sword gates by Christopher Werner. They may possibly be leftover pieces from the ironwork of the now-vanished Guard House, whose similar grilles are now at the Citadel, Charleston's famous military school.

Remarkably enough, this splendid ballroom still has its original cream and gilt paint. The stucco-work of the cornice, elaborate white marble mantel and the original gilt mirrors are indications of the scale of formal entertaining in early 19th-century Charleston.

TRADD STREET

The Colonel John Stuart House

One of the most charming of Charleston's thoroughfares, despite the intrusion upon it of towering, ugly telephone poles, is Tradd Street, which cuts across the old city from East Bay to the Ashley River. Among its gracious residences, none is finer than the Colonel John Stuart House, whose sunlit façade appears on the preceding page. Colonel Stuart came to Charleston from Scotland and built this handsome house with distinguished pedimented windows and door in 1772. He did not enjoy his fine home for long, as he was forced to flee to Florida in 1775 because of his Loyalist sympathies, but his wife continued to live here alone. The present owners have lavished great care on the interior. Their finest accomplishment is the grand and colorful drawing room shown on the color frontispiece.

(Left) The woodwork in the library is an exact reproduction of the original now in the Minneapolis Institute of Arts. The ornaments on the mantel include three Chinese export plates from a large family set.

The portrait of the mustachioed gentleman in the library is one of many family portraits in the house. This room also contains its share of inherited antiques. The curtains are ornamentally draped from gilt poles of the Greek revival period.

The dining room is painted an unusual mauve grey. Two Chippendale chairs with pierced vertical splats came from a Maryland plantation. The mantel clock is by Eli Terry of New England. The bow-front chest with its original brasses *(below)* is one of the finest antiques in the house.

*The Colonel John
Stuart House*

Under a section of a Buddhist altar screen is a seafaring ancestor's liqueur chest which has made many trips around the Horn.

This group of silver includes an urn and coffeepot (early works of Samuel Kirk of Baltimore) and a George III coffeepot.

The Colonel John Stuart House

The superb woodwork of the upstairs drawing room is exactly reproduced from the original now at the Minneapolis Institute.

The remarkably handsome Georgian chimney breast is beautifully hand-carved. The mantel is marble-white against grey walls.

The drawing room (*above* and *opposite*) stretches across the entire front of the house, with windows on three sides. Grey walls, gold hangings, white, rose and yellow upholstery, and ornamental touches of green and Chinese red are combined in a spontaneous but masterful color scheme.

At one end of the room is an early 18th-century highboy from Baltimore. The portrait on the left is a copy of a Sully. The one on the right, by the early American painter Hesselius, is of John Hanson, first president of the United States Congress in 1781.

The Colonel John Stuart House

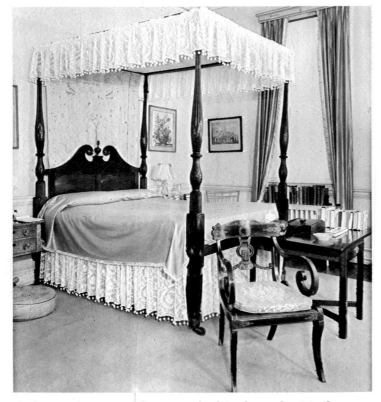

A fine 18th-century four-post bed is dressed with flounces of patterned net and ball fringe. The painted American Empire chair is one of a complete set.

The paneling in this same room is austerely simple, relieved only by a delicate dentil on the mantel. The small sofa is Victorian.

The Joseph Winthrop House

This is another of the several houses built in Charleston by New Englanders. Joseph Winthrop bore a distinguished Northern name, and a down-to-earth Yankee sense of business may have led him to Charleston which was becoming a prosperous seaport in post-Revolutionary days. He married a sister of the Charleston miniaturist, Charles Fraser, and raised a sizable family in this Tradd Street home which he built, in about 1797, on a plot of land belonging to his wife.

(Right) The downstairs drawing room has simple woodwork of the early 19th century. The portrait by Scarborough is of Mrs. David McCord. This remarkable lady was a well-known writer who also managed her family plantation and was a devoted worker in a Columbia hospital for Confederate wounded.

The living room on the second floor also has woodwork of restrained detail and is invitingly filled with books and family souvenirs. The portrait of the fine-looking gentleman was painted by Trumbull in 1806. It is of the owner's great-grandfather, John Tyrrell.

On the dining room mantel are grouped a harmonious collection of Oriental objects gathered during the owner's years of travel as a naval officer: a rose medallion teapot and plates, a pair of Chinese export mugs, and Chinese lamps of effective simplicity.

Old mahogany, family silver, and the brilliance of Oriental prints and porcelains are set off by a background of pure white walls. The three Chinese plates on the Irish Hepplewhite sideboard are rose medallion, and the drop-leaf table is Sheraton.

*The Humphrey
Sommers
House*

Little is known about the fine pre-Revolutionary house at 128 Tradd Street, except that it was built by Humphrey Sommers, probably in the 1770's. The large, beveled panels and bold moldings of the interior resemble those of other Charleston houses of that period. Its drawing room mantelpiece is an imposing *tour de force*. Handsome rococo carving decorates the well-studied architectural forms. Sturdy consoles with carved leaves support the mantelshelf. Above, the center panel is ingeniously tied into the broken pediment which, with a final flourish, houses an urn and festoons of bell flowers.

The Colonel Charles Pinckney House

On Orange Street, a few doors north of the corner of Tradd, is this engaging old house built by Colonel Charles Pinckney, a member of the large clan of Charleston Pinckneys. It was erected soon after 1769. As in a number of other double houses of the period, the facade extends upward into a handsome center pediment in the roof. A small, round window and dentil cornice moldings are the traditional last touches.

In the drawing room, the large wall panels of native cypress have been rubbed down to their natural tone. The mantelpiece is very simply worked, with the overmantel and its Georgian broken pediment indicated in a sort of architectural shorthand by the application of moldings.

The Colonel Charles Pinckney House — The décor of this room is subdued, with colors in the carpet, curtains and upholstery blending chromatically with the mellow tan of natural cypress. The placement of the furniture is deliberately spacious and uncluttered. Against the far wall is a fine 18th-century slant-top desk.

A small English corner stand in the Sheraton style holds a Sheffield urn which came from Hampton Plantation. The graceful lacquered chair is early Victorian.

When closed, this English Chippendale piece with handsome brasses appears to be a classic chest-on-chest, but one drawer opens out into a well-appointed writing shelf.

The William Elliott House

A few steps north of the point where Tradd Street crosses King Street is this single house with the typical solid lines of a very early building. Only a few houses as old as this one remain in Charleston. William Elliott apparently built it sometime before 1739, as a city map of that date indicates the house already constructed on this lot. The Elliott daughters became Mrs. Lewis Morris and Mrs. Daniel Huger, well-known Charleston names which in future generations became connected with fine mansions of later epochs. The present owners of the William Elliott House have delighted in retaining its early character and have carefully restored its livable old rooms.

The dining room is painted its original shade of pale grey-blue. The Sadler tiles were found when the fire-place was uncovered; they were probably installed by the Elliotts in the 1750's, when Sadler & Green of Liverpool first began making tiles decorated by the transfer method.

The drawing room is painted the original grey, set off by the Chinese red of the valences, Canton porcelains and the "fancy" chair by the fireplace. The portrait is of the owner's great-great-grandmother, seated in one of these very chairs, one of twelve made in Baltimore in 1812.

*The William
Elliott House*

The chaste library panels are painted a soft blue used at Williamsburg. The portrait is of the owner's great-great-*great*-grandfather.

An American Empire desk holds Chinese export cups and saucers, a rose medallion pitcher and mug, and a bronze and crystal candelabrum.

Judge Robert Pringle's house on Tradd Street was built in 1774, a fact known, for once, with considerable certainty, as the builder conveniently marked the date on the construction itself. This chimney breast is an example of the dignified style of the house. Its Georgian lines are bold and complete, and unadorned except for a simple strip of handsome wood carving under the mantelshelf.

The Judge Robert Pringle House

ALONG THE BAY SHORE

The William Gibbes House

Our path now follows a winding course along the shore of the old Charleston peninsula. Beginning with the William Gibbes House at South Battery, shown on the preceding page, it will wind eastward to the water's edge and then northward to the restored area known as Rainbow Row. The William Gibbes House is not only one of the finest in Charleston; it should be appreciated as a monument of Georgian architecture of national importance. William Gibbes probably began to build it soon after 1772. At the time that he lived in the house, a long wharf extended from the grounds into the Ashley River, whose bank was approximately where the far side of the street is today. Though the house has gone through many changes and restorations, very little, if any serious harm has been done to it. It has, in fact, acquired some of the very best features of periods that followed the time of its building.

(Left) The staircase in the main hall has a slender handrail and iron balusters. This doorway, one of four leading to the principal rooms, has a distinctive Adam cornice with oval corner rosettes added to the original Georgian frame.

A long view of the hall shows its impressive dimensions, divided midway by marbleized columns. The green, dark brown and rose pictorial paper is a copy of Zubor's *El Dorado,* a design first made in 1848. Below the landing are a tall-case clock and a Chinese lacquer screen.

The fine Georgian façade is distinguished by a doorway with side-lights and pilasters, surmounted by a wide entablature and pediment. The window treatment and the great roof pediment supported by consoles resemble those of many Georgian double houses, but here they are on a grander scale than usual. The double marble stairway rising to the main entrance above the foundation was added in about 1800. It was also at this time that a great deal of very fine decoration in the Adam style was added to the interior. One of the recent owners of the house, Mrs. Washington A. Roebling, lengthened the rooms in the rear of the house, restored the interior and filled it with fine period furniture.

(Right) Mrs. Roebling collected Chinese *objets d'art* and had one room on the first floor decorated in the Chinese Chippendale style as a background for them. Framed in the carved doorway of the Chinese Room is a section of the pictorial paper in the hall, above a carved Empire sofa.

The William Gibbes House

The Chinese painting over the mantelpiece is an ancestor portrait. The figures on the mantelshelf are glazed green and orange and resemble tomb figures of the T'ang dynasty. The woodwork of the room is water-green with panels of Chinese paper; the upholstery is deep apricot.

In a corner of the morning room stands a very unusual English walnut desk of the Queen Anne period. The hooded top and swelling lines indicate Dutch influence.

The mantelpiece in the guest room is another example of Adam décor added to an earlier room. Next to it stands an oval pole screen embroidered in needlepoint.

A downstairs bedroom for occasional guests is an early tradition in large houses like this one. The Empire mirror over the mantel is decorated with an elaborate relief of the car of Dionysus drawn by lions. The windows are curtained in *toile de Jouy*.

The William Gibbes House

The dining room was enlarged about twenty years ago. Its Adam mantel came from another Charleston house and is part of the restorations made in 1800. Among the many antiques are a Hepplewhite drop-leaf dining table with rounded extensions, and Hepplewhite shield-back chairs.

*The William
Gibbes House*

A small chest of drawers of the Queen Anne period has patterned, walnut veneer, its original brasses and extending drop leaves.

Phoenix birds perch on the frame of a rococo Chippendale mirror. The table with reeded legs is in the style of Duncan Phyfe.

The William Gibbes House

The great ballroom on the second floor is a breath-taking sight. The light of its many windows reflects iridescently from the immense Aubusson carpet to the high, coved ceiling, and the magnificent chandelier glitters with a fountain-spray of crystal. The walls are a warm grey, the curtains gold damask, the brocaded furniture pale rose and blue. At the end the of the room stands an old English harp made by Sebastien Eraros of London. The elaborately decorated Venetian harpsichord was once owned by Lady Barrington, who is said to have persuaded Paderewski to play upon it. The ceiling was recently redecorated in pure Adam style, with plaster medallions and corner fans touched with gold. The chairs and sofas are French Louis XVI, the portraits are by Sully, the mirrors are 18th-century English. Though the ensemble is international, it is probably Charleston's most perfectly harmonious example of Adam decoration in the grand manner.

The mantel in the ballroom has stucco reliefs of classic figures, a marble facing and a detailed molding to frame the overmantel. A close-up of this kind demonstrates in miniature how elaborate yet serene the best of Adam design can be.

The William Gibbes House

At the left is a detail of a pilaster on the frame of the ballroom doorway. Next to it is one of a matched pair of Chippendale mirrors of asymmetrical design.

This is one of a remarkable pair of French Empire card tables said to have belonged to the Emperor Nalopeon. They have dolphin feet under carved-eagle pedestals.

*The William
Gibbes House*

The French 18th-century bookcase, or *vitrine,* is of unpainted, bleached wood. It holds pieces of old glass, Chinese exportware, antique fans and leather-bound books. The pair of Louis XV chairs at either side still has the original blue and gold paint.

The carving of the bookcase is a combination of pilasters and moldings with rosettes, sprays and tiny pineapples of Louis XVI design.

This vivid portrait, dated 1814, is one of several in the room by Thomas Sully, the distinguished American who painted in Charleston for many years.

The Miles Brewton House

Near the crossing of King Street and South Battery stands a beautiful brick Georgian house with extensive gardens and with outbuildings that have hardly changed since slave days. The wealthy merchant Miles Brewton built this house soon after 1765. It is not known who was his architect, but Ezra Waite, a "joiner-architect" from London, made it plain that he did the woodwork. When an unscrupulous rival suggested that Ezra Waite had really had very little to do with the house, Waite published, in 1769, an indignant retort "begging leave to do himself justice." He had, he stated, "carved all the said work in the four principal rooms, also calculated, adjusted and draw'd at large for to work by, the Ionick entablature, and carved the same in front and round the eaves." Waite challenged contradiction to the tune of one hundred guineas for anyone who could disprove him, and there the matter still rests. Soon after, Miles Brewton and his entire family were lost at sea. The house went to his sister, Mrs. Jacob Motte. During the Revolution it was used as a headquarters by General Sir Henry Clinton. There are many stories of Mrs. Motte's tact and fortitude while acting as captive hostess to the British officers. She is said to have put so little trust in these gentlemen that she kept her daughters locked in the attic with their nurse.

Aaron Burr gave the bust of Napoleon on the drawing room mantel to Mrs. Motte's son-in-law, a man named Alston whose son, Joseph Alston, later governor of the state, married the beautiful Theodosia Burr. She, by a sad coincidence, was also lost at sea, while traveling to see her father returned from exile.

The Miles Brewton House

The architectural glories of the house center on the great drawing room which has a high, coved ceiling, an elaborate cornice, pedimented doors and this handsome chimney piece. The mantel is carved marble and above it the interesting wooden panel is designed with fluted pilasters and a broken pediment. In the panel hangs a portrait of Miles Brewton by Sir Joshua Reynolds. The Chippendale chair on the right is one of a set of twelve originally made for the room when it was used as a banquet hall. The phenomenal crystal chandelier was made for the house when it was built and is hung from the roof above the coved ceiling by a complicated system of steel cables.

The chandelier has remained miraculously intact for two centuries, in spite of wars, earthquakes and the recent collapse of ceiling decorations. These crashed to the floor, missed the chandelier by inches on all sides, and left every prism and hurricane shade untouched.

*The Miles
Brewton House*

The John Ashe House

Records indicate that the John Ashe House on South Battery was built some time between the Revolution and 1784. In a local advertisement of that year, a carpenter looking for work identified himself as the apprentice of a builder named Miller, pointing out with evident pride that this gentleman was responsible for the John Ashe House. Its roof is topped by a lantern, or cupola, which would be a familiar feature to a New Englander, but which is rare in Charleston. In the 1930's a number of alterations were made, with care, however, and a chimney was moved to an outside wall in order to enlarge the rooms inside. The woodwork required to finish the altered rooms was copied from the original.

The Hepplewhite card table between the windows in the drawing room, the corner cabinet and the handsome English secretary are all fine antiques. The ceiling cornice is interestingly designed to form the capitals of pilasters bordering door and window frames.

Under a distinguished cornice in the hall are folding doors with reeded ovals in each panel. Beyond is the chimney that was moved to enlarge the drawing room.

The little sitting room has the combination of styles so frequently seen in Charleston: early, sturdy wainscots and dentil cornices, and a later Adam mantel.

At the back of the spacious hall are two handsome architectural doorways. The paneled staircase is straight at the bottom and sweeps into a curve in the stairwell.

A pair of deep-blue and gold Meisson urns decorates the mantel in the sitting room. The Adam detail is typical of late 18th-century redecoration in Charleston.

The John Ashe House   The overmantel in the drawing room frames an Italian landscape. The Sèvres figurines represent soldiers of Napoleon's armies. The colonnettes and stucco details of the mantel are strikingly similar to those of other Charleston mantels of the period.

The General William Washington House

This comfortable house on South Battery, at the end of Church Street, was built by Thomas Savage in about 1768. General William Washington, by whose name it is usually known, was a kinsman of George Washington. He first came to Charleston as a cavalry officer during the Revolution, with "a small body of horse from Virginia." He married one of the many Charleston Elliotts during the war, and bought this house a few years after the British evacuated the city.

The dining room has wide paneling of the pre-Revolutionary period and damask curtains with elegantly draped valences. The ample Sheraton sideboard holds knife boxes and an urn-shaped wine cooler. The dining table from Virginia and the set of Sheraton chairs are family pieces.

The spacious drawing room is also furnished with family pieces, including a sofa, at the left, and several armchairs, all from the Pinckney family's famous Parisian *vernis Martin* sets. The portrait of the owner, over the Empire card table against the far wall, is by Irving Wiles.

The General William Washington House

The mantelpiece in the library is designed with severe and forceful Georgian lines. The revolving drum table at the left is Sheraton. The small pedestal table at the right is considered unusual for having four rather than three gracefully curved legs.

The Robert William Roper House

The Robert William Roper House (*c.* 1838) is a brick, Greek revival building of outspoken grandeur. The two-story portico with immense white columns is very nearly theatrical, but it indicates accurately the fashionable way of life of the wealthy planters of its day. The house stands on the Battery and commands a magnificent view of the harbor and the sea. It was built shortly after the Battery sea wall was erected to protect this part of the low-lying city from tides and flood. Originally the house must have been furnished with many fine pieces of furniture. The present owner, a descendant of plantation families, has carried the tradition to this day; in the house now, are pieces that once furnished the old mansion at Magnolia, the plantation on the Ashley River whose beautiful gardens are one of the showplaces of the state. Inside, the scale of the house is as grand as the exterior leads one to expect, especially on the second floor, where the rooms, planned primarily for entertaining, have dramatically high ceilings and tall windows and doors.

The wide door leading from the drawing room to the dining room is very delicately designed for this late period. Both rooms have grey walls and identically draped turquoise hangings. The mantels are of black marble. The chandeliers and sconces were originally made for the house.

The Robert William Roper House   The Sheraton table, chairs and sideboard in the dining room are all English. The silver service on the sideboard belonged to Dr. John Grimke Drayton, creator of the Magnolia gardens. The fine George I silver cup on the table came from the Old Field Plantation.

In this view from the dining room into the drawing room, the imposing height of the double doorway is emphasized by two small 18th-century candlestands at either side, holding exquisite early-Victorian bouquets of shell flowers under glass bells.

The Robert William
Roper House

A fine upholstered American Chippendale chair is placed in a corner of the drawing room. The Chinese chessmen in the shelves above belonged to Dr. Drayton.

This drop-leaf pedestal table is American Sheraton and has an unusually shaped top. The two painted and gilded Sheraton chairs came from the Miles Brewton House.

The James Hartley House

This white house on East Battery, gleaming in the Southern sun, with its green blinds and shady piazzas, is as typical of Charleston as any house one could find. This area was burnt out by the great fire of 1740, and records show that James Hartley built here some years later, probably in 1755. In the manner of the classic single house, the piazzas with a street entrance at one end were added later. Originally, the central window was a door to the sidewalk.

This house contains much original Georgian paneling. In the drawing room, only the mantel is a restoration. This room may have been the office of an early occupant named John Fraser, head of an export firm that grew to be financial representative of the Confederacy to England.

The charming second-floor living room has slate-blue woodwork, white plaster walls and white linen slipcovers and curtains. The tile facing of the fireplace is almost entirely original. Over the mantel is a portrait of the owner's grandfather.

The paneled end of the dining room is all original except the mantel which is an excellent reproduction of Georgian design. The china cabinets with keystone arches and glass-paned doors are fine examples of the period that have been used as models for restorations in other houses.

The Inglis' Arch House

Rainbow Row is a strip of charming old houses on East Battery, once considered the finest water front on the Atlantic seaboard. As time passed, the harbor shore line receded, a number of fires devastated the quarter and businesses moved away. Rainbow Row became picturesquely, but decrepitly, a slum. It inspired the original setting of DuBose Heyward's novel, and George Gershwin's opera, *Porgy and Bess*—a distinguished role for any row of houses to play, though decades of destructive wear and tear had to precede it. In recent years, enterprising Charlestonians have rescued Rainbow Row from disintegration and recreated one of the most delightful residential areas in the city. Originally, it was inhabited by merchants who lived on the upper floors of the houses, while business was transacted below. The Inglis' Arch House, built by George Inglis in about 1778, takes its name from the arch on the ground floor that leads from the Battery to a narrow street beyond. The present owners of the house made a great contribution to the preservation of old Charleston by purchasing and rehabilitating five other houses on Rainbow Row.

The low-ceilinged dining room is painted a deep, emerald green with pure white trim, an effective background for a pair of crystal sconces, two Goya prints and Chinese exportware arranged on a hanging shelf. The chairs are Chippendale ladder-backs.

Mirrors in the recesses on either side of the fireplace enlarge the dining room. A French *trumeau* hangs over the English sideboard. The red tôle lamps are French.

A collection of old pewter—a large charger, a bowl, candlesticks and tankards—is grouped on a table in the small hallway, under a set of colorful bird prints.

In the little sitting room, dark Pompeian-red walls are set off by light trim. Here are a number of French Directoire pieces, several paintings from the owner's collection of contemporary art, and a variety of amusing carved ornaments, some English and some Mexican.

The Inglis'
Arch House

118

The tall fruitwood secretary in the drawing room is unusually designed and may be Italian, though the lower section is of Louis XVI inspiration.

This diminutive French cabinet is thought to have come from a chalet that belonged to Madame de Pompadour. The platters on the wall brackets are Chinese exportware.

*The Inglis'
Arch House*

The drawing room is furnished with many other French pieces, including the painted-canvas Directoire screen, now divided in two. The Leeds plates under the mantelshelf are decorated with the coat of arms of Christopher Columbus. The contemporary painting above is by Etienne Ret.

The Colonel Othniel Beale House

A few steps north along Rainbow Row is the house whose owners were the first to venture a restoration on the old water front. The Colonel Othniel Beale House was built in about 1740 by a New Englander from Marblehead, Massachusetts. Othniel Beale was an engineer in charge of the fortifications of the city at the time of the fire of 1740 which devastated this area. The rear of this very building was the model for the set in the first production of *Porgy and Bess*.

Despite years of neglect, the cypress paneling in the house was found practically intact. In the library it has been rubbed down to the natural wood and set off by turquoise plaster walls. The mid-18th-century card table with cabriole legs, in the foreground, is a very fine piece.

The Colonel Othniel Beale House

The house is rich in Charleston-made pieces and other South Carolina antiques. In the drawing room, the Queen Anne "handkerchief" table, on the right, is an unusual example: it has a top only twenty inches square and a swinging leg under a diagonal drop leaf.

The oval, pembroke tea table at the left is a fine piece in the Hepplewhite style, made in Charleston for the owner of Ophir Plantation. The armchair is Sheraton.

The large Brunswick Star platter among these old porcelains belonged to an ancestor of the owner, Dr. John Bachman, a great friend and collaborator of Audubon.

The blue-grey drawing room woodwork is of the same design as that in the library beyond. Rice in the vases on the Sheraton secretary is a souvenir from the last family plantation. The open card table is very fine American Chippendale. The unusual fire screen opens out into a desk.

The Colonel Othniel Beale House

The remarkable dining room table has a tilt top made of a single piece of mahogany. The Hepplewhite sideboard is Charleston-made.

The steep, narrow stairs have their original 18th-century, turned balusters and heavy handrail. The Audubon prints in the stair well belonged to Dr. Bachman.

The Daniel Bourget House

Just north of Rainbow Row is Elliott Street, which was cut inland from the bay to divide one of the inconveniently large blocks of the original Charleston city plan of 1672. It became a prosperous business and shopping street before the Revolution, but after the fire of 1778 it was never the same again. Elliott Street was sadly neglected during the 19th century, but the enthusiasm for restoration has spread through the quarter and a number of its small houses have come to life again. Daniel Bourget was the builder of one of them, probably in 1741. The interior was evidently damaged by more than one fire and it was rebuilt within the same walls in the late 18th century.

(Right) The second-floor drawing room has walls painted the pale grey-green of celadon china. Curtains and upholstery are oyster white. This handsome English Hepplewhite secretary-bookcase, made before 1790, contains old English porcelains. The Hepplewhite armchair is one of a set of twelve made in Philadelphia for Edward Rutledge, a member of the Continental Congress and a signer of the Declaration of Independence.

The dining room has pale apricot walls and stylized curtains of a deeper tone. The late Sheraton table with rope-twist legs came from Nantucket. The fine crystal chandelier is in scale with the small room. The painting over the mantel is by Selinger of Munich, dated 1879.

The Gibbs-Blackwood House

When the Gibbs-Blackwood House was bought by the present owners, it was occupied by no less than seven tenement families. It took a full year to establish this horde of people in the big Federal housing projects in other parts of Charleston, before work could begin on what is now a most original and attractive house. It was built by George Gibbs who bought the lot in 1793. His daughter Caroline Blackwood also lived in the house for some years and the family prospered here until after the War of 1812.

(Left) The kitchen is decorated as a room to be lived in. The mantelpiece is a restoration; the horse in the 19th-century painting above was a trotter that belonged to the owner's grandfather. The highboy, which is from Boston, the painted Hitchcock chairs and the Sheraton table are good pieces in a very exceptional kitchen.

The dining room walls are partly rough plaster and partly covered with their original simple sheathing. The table is 16th- or 17th-century French, the chairs Spanish. The sideboard belonged to Sir George Gray, first governor of New Zealand. On it is a large Chinese export tureen.

The Joseph Manigault House

Broad Street, running from east to west across the city, serves in this chapter as a dividing line between old Charleston and the larger area to the north. This division is somewhat arbitrary, for fine houses of the past are scattered "north of Broad Street" in a quantity that would be considered exceptional in most American cities. The charming gate-house pavilion shown on the preceding page is what remains of the outbuildings of a fine mansion on Ashmead Place, the Joseph Manigault House. The house itself dates from 1803. It was designed for Joseph Manigault by his brother Gabriel, Charleston's best-known amateur architect, who studied in Europe and introduced the Adam style to the city. In 1933, the Manigault House and the gardens around it were generously given to the Charleston Museum.

(Left) Gabriel Manigault's designs for the cornice, mantel and doorframes in the dining room are elegant examples of Adam decoration. The dining table is late Sheraton.

The wide bay at one end of the room is typical of an Adam interior. The two tilt-top tables and the chairs are a set, probably Charleston-made; each piece is inlaid with a silver plaque bearing the crest of the Mathews family, descendants of a Revolutionary governor of the state.

The Joseph Manigault House

The donor of the house also presented to the Museum this fabulous chandelier hanging in the well of the free-flying staircase.

The drawing room has architectural doorframes with pairs of engaged columns and a coved ceiling with an elaborate cornice.

The Manigault House is safely watched over by the Museum, but still more public support will be needed to complete its restoration. The drawing room mantel, though not intact, is as handsome as ever. The columns on each side are variations of those used on the doorframes.

The coved ceiling in the drawing room has painted decorations of a later date than the rest of the room. The pair of pedestal tables flanking the mantel are Sheraton; the Hepplewhite shield-back chairs are also a pair. The portrait, painted in 1757 by the Charleston artist, Jeremiah Theus, is of Mrs. Peter Manigault, mother of Joseph and Gabriel.

The Joseph Manigault House

The Philip Porcher House

Philip Porcher built this house on Archdale Street in about 1765. The wooden construction on a high, brick foundation resembles the plantation houses of its time, rather than a city house. Though it has changed hands a number of times, it is again in the family and is owned by one of Philip Porcher's descendants. The owner of this house is exceptionally well-surrounded with family history, for across the street stands the Lutheran church established by still another antecedent, Dr. John Bachman, who was pastor there for forty-eight years. The American primitive portrait in the drawing room *(below)* of the Philip Porcher House is of Dr. Bachman's mother.

The drawing room still has all its original large, beveled panels. The delicate fanlight in the arched doorway was added some time after 1800. The small Queen Anne table (*c.* 1750) against the wall, with straight legs and pad feet, is typical of early Charleston-made furniture.

The Colonel William Rhett House

This beautiful house was built in 1712 by Colonel William Rhett on what was then a plantation outside the city limits. It may well be the oldest dwelling in Charleston. Colonel Rhett was vice-admiral of the Province and remains famous in South Carolina for his capture of Stede Bonnet, a notorious pirate who for years prowled the Carolina coast. The house now stands on Hasell Street, but originally it faced an avenue of its own that led into the city. The handsome double entrance steps and their iron railings are recent additions which lead to piazzas on both sides of the house. This is the birthplace of Lieutenant-General Wade Hampton, cavalry hero of Lee's army, Governor of South Carolina and United States Senator.

(Opposite) The dining room has a rare type of plaster decoration in white on the powder-blue walls. The festoons over the windows are of 18th-century classic style. The screen at the left is covered with silk painted with Chinese designs similar to those of 18th-century wallpapers.

The remarkable wall ornamentation is of the earliest period of stucco decoration in America, shortly after 1750. The family portrait on the left is of John Watts de Peyster; the other is of Lord Bellamont, Crown Governor of New York before the Revolution.

The rococo overmantel which now frames a 17th-century Dutch portrait is part of the early wall decorations in the dining room.

This Chippendale group at the end of the room includes a fine gilt mirror and an American card table with cabriole legs.

The incised decorations of the chair rail and cornice in the living room were probably installed in about 1800. The tasseled valences are of brilliantly painted antique silk. The secretary on the right is 18th-century English, with delicate fretwork in the base and pediment.

A carefully considered group·on one wall combines early and modern paintings with an English Chinese Chippendale wall clock. Two Venetian blackamoors form the bases of the pair of lamps. The comfortable modern sofa adapts itself gracefully to the company of *bibelots* and antiques.

The Colonel William Rhett House

The Empire mantel made of several kinds of marble came from another Charleston house. Above it is a Chippendale landscape mirror.

The English Queen Anne reading chair is a very rare piece. It is meant to be straddled and the back is used as an arm rest.

Ashley Hall

Early in the 1800's, buildings began to appear along what is now Rutledge Avenue, in a fashionable suburb called Cannonsboro that is well within the city limits today. It has been suggested that Ashley Hall was built here by an English architect named William Jay, who was in Charleston from 1819 to 1822. The house is in his Regency style. But research has since proposed an earlier date for Ashley Hall, about 1816. The true architect's name is not known, but the house was built for an Englishman named Patrick Duncan who sold it some thirteen years later. Among Ashley Hall's occupants have been George A. Trenholme, Secretary of the Treasury of the Confederacy, and Charles Otto Witte, Consul of the German Empire, who extended and improved the magnificent gardens. Architecturally, the house is a classic villa, but on a very grand scale. The imposing columned portico stands on its own arcaded, stone foundation which is now glassed-in to form a conservatory in front of the main entrance. Ashley Hall was once known as the James Nicholson House, after an early owner, and was renamed by the girls' preparatory school which now occupies it.

Many of the mantelpieces in Ashley Hall are not as old as the house itself, but the white marble one in the sitting room is original. The basket of fruit in the center panel is carved in high relief and the grooved pilasters are finished with elaborate, curved acanthus leaves.

Ashley Hall

(Right) Ashley Hall shows the Empire and Regency influence that followed the Federal period. Yet the character of the columns, pilasters and door panels in the drawing room, and of its vaults and flattened arches could also be classified as very late Federal without searching for foreign names. In any case, this finely detailed room represents a certain peak in 19th-century American architecture and workmanship.

On the ornamentally vaulted staircase landing are doors with Greek revival moldings and corner rosettes, bowed to follow the curved walls of adjoining rooms.

On the inside, the curved doorway of the sitting room has pilasters with modified acanthus capitals and an entablature with festoons of an earlier classic style.

The Dock Street Theatre

One of the most delightful corners of Charleston is a section of Church Street where several historic public buildings are gathered together— St. Philip's and the Huguenot Church, and the picturesque Planters' Hotel seen here from the old Huguenot Cemetery. During the 18th century, the Planters' Hotel was patronized by plantation families when they came to the city to do business. The Dock Street Theatre, directly behind it on Dock Street (now Queen Street) was their place of entertainment. It opened in 1736. Recently, the theatre, of which only the walls remained, and the hotel were restored together, so that the theatre entrance is now on Church Street through the old hotel. The new Dock Street Theatre was dedicated in November, 1937, with a production of *The Recruiting Officer,* an ancient drama which had been the original theatre's opening-night offering.

The ground floor of the Planters' Hotel is now the Dock Street Theatre lobby. Above it is a handsome reception room, reconstructed with fine Adam mantelpieces and woodwork from the old Radcliffe House, now destroyed, which dated from about 1802.

A ceiling centerpiece of excellent Adam design was installed in the reception room which is used between the acts as a gathering place for the theatre audience.

The Dock Street Theatre

(Above) This remarkable doorway which leads into the reception room is pure Adam in inspiration. The delicate designs may have been made by William Purvis, a very fine stucco craftsman who is known to have been working in Charleston when the Radcliffe House was built.

(Right) The restoration of the Dock Street Theatre was a particularly imaginative W.P.A. project. Without it, such fine relics as this old mantel, somewhat battered by the years, might have vanished altogether.

The Governor Thomas Bennett House

In a suburb once known as Harleston, Thomas Bennett, Sr. acquired land on the west side of the Charleston peninsula where he used tidal water power for his lumber mills. This gentleman was a contractor who took a great interest in architecture and the development of his city. He designed a number of interesting buildings including the Orphan House and a rice mill at James Island. His son, Thomas Bennett, Jr., became governor of South Carolina, but found time in spite of politics to take the same interest in architecture that his father had. In 1825, he built this substantial mansion on his father's land, overlooking the family mill. The city has long since grown up around the Governor Thomas Bennett House and it now stands on Lucas Street.

The hall woodwork is in the transitional style of the 1820's. The wainscot and the entablature above the door are of the classic era; the beaded inserts and square medallions of the doorframe are of a later design.

The doorframes and ceiling cornices in the hallways are fittingly elaborate for a governor's mansion. Under the keystone arch of the rear stair hall are a doorway and fanlight which were originally in an upper hall.

Mrs. Jane Wightman's House

This Greek revival house on Chalmers Street was finished in 1840 and has recently been restored by a member of the Pinckney family. This view of it through one of the decorative iron gates of Washington Square also shows one of the few remaining cobbled streets in the city. The entrance door and piazzas are later additions and the wrought-iron balcony, from an old house nearby, is part of the recent restoration. The house contains many interesting Pinckney family pieces, including some *vernis Martin* furniture which an observant visitor to Charleston will note is a recurring theme in the homes of Pinckney descendants all over the city. This furniture was imported from Paris by an ancestor of the owner of this house, General Charles Cotesworthy Pinckney. It is in the style of the Martin brothers who developed a method of decorating with painted designs and panels in imitation of oriental lacquer. General Pinckney discovered the furniture on the occasion of a diplomatic mission to the French Directorate in 1797. The mission became known as the XYZ Affair and was a signal failure, but it did produce the famous slogan "Millions for defense, sir, but not one cent for tribute."

The late Sheraton dining table and the Chippendale chairs all came from the Pinckney family plantation. The gold and blue curtains, draped in a charmingly conventional Empire design, came from the home of Chief Justice Pinckney on East Bay, which was destroyed in the fire of 1861.

Over the dining room mantel hangs a portrait of the owner's ancestor, General Charles Cotesworth
Pinckney. It is by James Earle who settled in Charleston in 1794 and painted a number of excellent
portraits of distinguished Charlestonians before his death two years later.

Mrs. Jane
Wightman's House

At the top of a dining room wall cabinet is a pierced gilt French Empire fruit dish. Below it are a Meisson chocolate set and a Chelsea pierced fruit dish.

The mantel and woodwork in the entrance hall are original except for the arch at the right which is part of the recent alterations. The sofa is from the Pinckney *vernis Martin* set.

Mrs. Jane Wightman's House

The woodwork of the second-floor living room is all original except for the book shelves which occupy the recessed arches to very good effect. The porcelain urns on the top shelves are French. On the mantel stand a pair of Royal Worcester dishes and a blue Meisson urn.

The Gaillard-Bennett House

Theodore Gaillard probably built this handsome house on Montagu Street between 1800 and 1803, when this part of Charleston was still open country. It is an impressive building, both inside and out. The portico was probably added in the 1830's by a later owner; its columns with capitals of different designs, the dentil moldings of the pediment, and the decoration around the entrance door are distinguished and clearly the work of a fine architect. Inside, in almost every room, there is plaster-work decorating the mantels, ceilings and cornices which surpasses anything of this period remaining in Charleston. In 1851, the house was bought by Washington Jefferson Bennett, son of Governor Thomas Bennett whose house stands not far away on Lucas Street.

(Opposite) The most extraordinary example of plasterwork in the house is in the drawing room where an intricate series of molded designs joins the overmantel to the decorated ceiling.

Undersea plants and shells decorate the central tablet of this remarkable drawing room mantel; the relief in several planes gives a striking illusion of perspective. Flanking the tablet are stucco molds representing fox-hunting scenes and over the fine double pilasters are two exquisite floral sprays, one of which is reproduced in detail on the copyright page.

142

In one bedroom, pointed arches, colonnettes and classic urns and sprays decorate a mantel different from any other in the house. The arches at either end, with shells under the points, are almost identical to those on the fox-and-hound mantel in the George Eveleigh House.

The Gaillard-Bennett House is unique in Charleston for the quantity and intricacy of the Adam décor that has survived there. The bedroom where this mantel stands is so richly ornamented, even for this house, as to suggest that it was intended as a reception room.

The Gaillard-Bennett House

NEIGHBORING
PLANTATIONS

Medway Plantation

Plantations were an integral part of Charleston life, and no treatise on the stately homes of Charleston would be complete without some mention of the handsome estates in the surrounding Low Country. Shown on the preceding page is Medway, the oldest of them all—a rambling house dwarfed by great oaks hung with Spanish moss which are the hallmark of a Carolina plantation. Medway was built by a Dutchman, Jan Van Arrsens, in about 1686, and it is probably the oldest house in South Carolina. Though it has gone through numerous alterations, it has kept its ancient, Low Country aspect. Its Dutch, stepped-gable ends are built of bricks made of clay from the banks of the Back River, originally known as the Medway, which flows just beyond the green lawns of Medway Plantation.

(Left) The 18th-century paneling in the drawing room is of native cypress and came from a neighboring plantation. A pair of T'ang horses dating from about 1618 and two Persian bowls decorate the mantelshelf.

The owners of Medway have furnished their delightful house with a rare combination of classic antiques and exotic trophies brought back from expeditions to distant lands. The collection in the drawing room includes curios from Europe and from China, Nepal, Tibet, India and Persia.

Medway Plantation Between the book shelves that have been built into the panels of another wall is a charming shell niche which holds an old French tea set, Chinese export plates and 18th-century Persian pottery bowls. The armchair by the desk is English Chippendale.

At Halidon Hill Plantation, an old house is being restored which was recently moved to this site via woods, fields and country roads. The kitchen is modernly equipped and invitingly decorated with an original mantelpiece and furniture modeled after early designs. Old iron kitchen tools are placed by the fireplace which is occupied by a very up-to-date electric spit.

*Halidon
Hill
Plantation*

Middleton Place

The house at Middleton Place was destroyed in 1865, as were all the plantations along this bank of the Ashley River except Drayton Hall. The present house was built in what remained of the original south wing. The elder Henry Middleton, a notably prosperous planter who became president of the Continental Congress in 1774, created the remarkable gardens at Middleton Place. Their sweeping terraces, giant oaks and magnificent planting remain one of the first delights of South Carolina. Henry Middleton's grandson, also named Henry, was minister to Russia. Czar Nicholas I presented a portrait of himself to Ambassador Middleton which is still at the plantation in an interesting room furnished with his French Empire collection. Another grandson, John Izard Middleton, an archeologist and painter, seems to have enjoyed his wealth with more freedom and less responsibility. He associated with the European celebrities of the day and it is said that the portrait of Madame Récamier hanging in the drawing room today *(right)* was presented to him by that lady herself.

The French Empire furniture is painted with dark mahogany graining and skillful gilt decorations. The red damask curtains and sofa covering are original fabrics of the period. The small painting at the left is by Greuze. The prized portrait of Czar Nicholas hangs over the sofa.

Mulberry Plantation

The house at Mulberry Plantation was built on a high bluff above the western branch of the Cooper River in 1714. It is the only brick house of this period left in the area. The builder was Thomas Broughton, rice planter, Indian trader, one-time governor and, perhaps, something of an adventurer. It has been hinted that he acquired this property by the simple ruse of building his house before he owned the land—a choice plantation site which had been set aside for Lord Ashley Cooper. The house and its pavilions attached to the four corners have quaint roof lines of Jacobean inspiration. The name of the plantation came from an ancient mulberry tree that stood on the bluff when the Indians were still cultivating this fertile land.

The dining room has late 18th-century woodwork and a fine collection of old Sheraton furniture. The sideboard dates from before 1780. The portrait by Jeremiah Theus is of the builder's grandson, Alexander Broughton. The pavilion beyond the corner door is used as a breakfast room.

Mulberry Plantation Another view of the dining room shows the fireplace wall and a glimpse of the drawing room. The woodwork and mantelpieces of the two rooms are of deliberately similar design. The date of the house is established by figures cut in the iron weathervanes of the pavilions *(opposite)*.

In the recessed corner of the dining room, a blue and gold Rockingham tea set is displayed in a shell wall cabinet. The brass-bound case is an English cellaret.

This is one of two arrangements made at each side of the door with pairs of fine Sheraton card tables, bird paintings and silver candelabra.

By the door leading from the drawing room to the rear stair hall are an American banjo clock and a secretary-bookcase dating from the 1770's. The sideboard in the hall is English Hepplewhite. The early staircase has a simple, polished-wood wainscot.

Mulberry Plantation

Mulberry Plantation

(*Above*) A charming old harpsichord occupies the far corner of the drawing room. The wall cabinet is like the one in the dining room and holds parts of a pink lustreware tea set.

(*Right*) The front door at Mulberry opens directly into the drawing room which takes the place of a large central hall. Among its fine antiques are a pair of upholstered Chippendale armchairs and an English butler's tray that is unusual for its circular shape. The wall sconces are Baccarat crystal.

Seabrook House

A cotton planter named William Seabrook built this mansion on Edisto Island in about 1810. It is an unusually consistent example of the Federal style; the unverified legend is that Seabrook House was designed by Hoban, the Irish-born architect of the White House who worked for a while in Charleston. The double portico, with its pediment, slender columns, and flattened arches above, resembles others of the same period in the city. The double flight of steps leading to the porch gracefully disguises high foundations that are a practical necessity in the Low Country. The iron railing is decorated with William Seabrook's initials. Seabrook House stood for many years empty and neglected in the midst of the towering oaks of the deserted plantation. The present owners have completely restored it and have transformed the grounds with beautiful planting and gardens.

A splendid, flower-banked central hall runs through the house to the back garden. A wide arch in the middle allows a full view of the remarkable double staircase whose two sides join over the garden door. The delicate detail of the woodwork is high-lighted with two-tone painting.

Seabrook House — Seabrook House is decorated with a lively sense of color. The dining room walls are lined with a replica of an old paper in shades of deep gold and lavender. The woodwork is painted pale green and ivory. One of several family portraits in the house hangs over the mantel.

(Above, left) In the dining room, an English cabinet of contrasting polished woods conceals an electric plate warmer in one of its side cupboards. The two porcelain *pot-de-crème* sets still have their matching stands. The English bird print above is a black-and-white mezzotint of remarkable quality. The mahogany sideboard (above, right) with unusual shell inlays holds silver tankards and massive pieces of old English Davenport china.

(Left) The chairs are Sheraton and the side table at the far right is Hepplewhite. The Brussels tapestry carpet has a bold pattern of green leaves. The mass of daffodils and lavender stock on the table add a final stroke of color to this hospitable room.

Seabrook House

Seabrook House

(*Above*) The drawing room mantel is a charming example of the restrained design of the woodwork throughout the house. Of the many antiques with which Seabrook is furnished, none attracts such enthusiastic comment as the perambulator at the right; a Victorian mother would be startled to discover that the family baby carriage has been put to use as a rolling cocktail bar.

(*Right*) All manner of colors are confidently mingled in the drawing room with its document wallpaper, patterned fabrics, pictures, and flowered Brussels tapestry carpet. Masses of fresh flowers from the gardens brighten the rooms of this already cheerful house.

Drayton Hall

Drayton Hall brings this volume to a close with something of a flourish, for it is very probably the finest untouched example of Georgian architecture still standing in America. It has survived the years unblemished by gas, electricity or central heating. Though it was built in 1738, some of the original paint actually remains on its beautifully paneled walls. Antiquarians are in awe of this great house whose rooms present themselves today, nearly empty but magnificent, just as the architect conceived them. The original plan included two extensive wings that would widen and greatly improve the exterior proportions. This view shows the west front with a pedimented portico, extending only slightly forward, made spacious by deep reveals in the façade. The builder of Drayton Hall was the Honorable John Drayton whose son, William Henry Drayton, became a Revolutionary patriot and chief justice of his state. In 1865, Drayton Hall had providentially been turned into a hospital for smallpox victims. The Union troops were not tempted to set foot on the premises and Drayton Hall was saved from the systematic burning of the whole Ashley River area.

Some of Drayton Hall's old Georgian mantels were replaced by others in the Adam style in about 1800. This one in the original dining room contrasts with the deep-cut, 18th-century panels and is perhaps a discordant change, but it is a charming specimen of the type nevertheless.

Drayton Hall   The drawing room grandly demonstrates on what an ambitious scale John Drayton planned his
house. The elaborate plaster work of the ceiling is in astonishingly good condition. The doors are
framed with Ionic pilasters and heavy cornices, and more pilasters mark the corners of the room.
The original overmantel, rich with carving and a scrolled pediment, is intact. The exquisite mantel
below it is one of the Adam replacements.

This detail of the mantel in the drawing room shows what delicacy and refinement Adam decoration could achieve under the hand of a master craftsman. The formal bowl brims over with finely chiseled fruit and leaves, and the scrolls are drawn with unfaltering grace.

Drayton Hall

A marble-topped table originally made for Drayton Hall stands in the great hall beyond the drawing room. Its pair is now in the Heyward-Washington House in Charleston.

A rare feature of the drawing room is the carved mahogany decoration over each window. The small table is another original piece that has always been in the house.

Drayton Hall   The great hall on the first floor is massive in scale and unsymmetrical in plan. Its richly carved cornice, panels and chimney breast have never been tampered with. The overmantel was probably adapted from one of the designs of the famous English architect, Inigo Jones.

The double staircase outside the great hall was conceived with similar grandeur. The wooden balusters and carving remain unpainted, as they were intended to be.

In most fine houses, the less formal woodwork in this bedroom would be quite handsome enough for the drawing room. Wooden steps are still kept by the four-post bed.

The great hall is painted in two muted tones of blue. This second view of it shows its most extraordinary *Drayton Hall* feature—a plaster ceiling centerpiece whose oval decoration in high relief has remained intact for more than two centuries. The carved rosettes are repeated in the metopes of the ceiling cornice. A period room of this scale and authenticity has few parallels in America.

Drayton Hall   Above the great hall, the baronial second-floor drawing room is as imposing as its counterpart below. The principal fireplace is faced with marble and crowned by a crested overmantel that leaves one groping for superlatives. A pictorial treatise on the beauties of the Southern interiors of Charleston and its Low Country could do no better than to close on this exalted note.

INDEX

of Text and Captions

167